Follow Me Around™
Mexico

By Wiley Blevins

SCHOLASTIC

Content Consultant: Luis Urrieta Jr., PhD, Associate Professor, Mexican American Studies, Lozano Long Institute of Latin American Studies, University of Texas at Austin, Austin, Texas

Library of Congress Cataloging-in-Publication Data
Names: Blevins, Wiley, author.
Title: Mexico / by Wiley Blevins.
Description: New York : Children's Press, an imprint of Scholastic Inc., 2018. |
Series: Follow me around | Includes bibliographical references and index.
Identifiers: LCCN 2017004663 | ISBN 9780531237069 (library binding) | ISBN 9780531239728 (pbk.)
Subjects: LCSH: Mexico—Juvenile literature.
Classification: LCC F1208.5 .B57 2018 | DDC 972—dc23
LC record available at https://lccn.loc.gov/2017004663

Design: Judith Christ Lafond & Anna Tunick Tabachnik
Text: Wiley Blevins
© 2018 Scholastic Inc.

All rights reserved. Published in 2018 by Children's Press, an imprint of Scholastic Inc.
Printed in the United States of America 113
SCHOLASTIC, CHILDREN'S PRESS, and associated logos are trademarks and/or registered trademarks of Scholastic Inc., 557 Broadway, New York, NY 10012.

1 2 3 4 5 6 7 8 9 10 R 27 26 25 24 23 22 21 20 19 18

Photos ©: cover background: Jeremy Woodhouse/Getty Images; cover children: Ron Levine/Getty Images; back cover: Ron Levine/Getty Images; 1: Ron Levine/Getty Images; 3 background: Public Domain; 3 bottom right: Pixelrobot/Dreamstime; 4 background: Ron Levine/Getty Images; 6 left: Frank Fell/Getty Images; 6 right: Timothy Hearsum/Getty Images; 7 left: lenawurm/Getty Images; 7 right: mofles/Getty Images; 8 top: Edgardo Contreras/Getty Images; 8 center top: Juanmonino/Getty Images; 8 center bottom: John E. Kelly/Exactostock-1598/Superstock, Inc.; 8 bottom: alisafarov/Getty Images; 9 top: Ronaldo Schemidt/AFP/Getty Images; 9 center top: Dana Gallagher/Getty Images; 9 center bottom: Lisa Romerein/Getty Images; 9 bottom: Gentl and Hyers/Getty Images; 10: Robert Harding Productions/age fotostock; 12 bottom left: diegograndi/iStockphoto; 12-13 cartoons: Molesko Studio/Shutterstock; 12-13 background: Vadim Yerofeyev/Dreamstime; 14 left: John Coletti/AWL Images; 14 top right: Eye Ubiquitous/UIG/Getty Images; 14 bottom right: migstock/Alamy Images; 15 left: Danita Delimont/Alamy Images; 15 top right: stockcam/iStockphoto; 15 bottom right: CSP_billperry/age fotostock; 16: DEA/C SAPPA/age fotostock; 17 top left: Kobby Dagan/VWPics/age fotostock; 17 bottom left: Kevin Schafer/Alamy Images; 17 center: dbimages/Alamy Images; 17 right: David Parker/Alamy Images; 18 left: Felipe Davalos/National Geographic/Getty Images; 18 center: Maciej Czekajewski/Dreamstime; 18 right: The Granger Collection; 19 left: Everett Historical/Shutterstock; 19 right: Hermsdorf/iStockphoto; 20 bottom left: ithinksky/Getty Images; 20 center: Stootsy/Shutterstock; 20 top right: Maximilian Stock Ltd./Getty Images; 21 top: aldomurillo/iStockphoto; 21 bottom: Pixelrobot/Dreamstime; 22 top: Angela Ostafichuk/Shutterstock; 22 bottom: Richard Ellis/Alamy Images; 23 left: Jorge Silva/AFP/Getty Images; 23 top right: Richard Levine/age fotostock; 23 bottom right: ivanastar/iStockphoto; 24 top: CSA-Plastock/Getty Images; 24 bottom: VvoeVale/iStockphoto; 25: Franco Origlia/Getty Images; 26 left: vainillaychile/Getty Images; 26 right: Danita Delimont Stock/AWL Images; 26 bottom: Erin Patrice O'Brien/Getty Images; 27 top left: SOLOFOTOFOX/Thinkstock; 27 top right: Peter Donaldson/Alamy Images; 27 bottom: Luis Acosta/AFP/Getty Images; 28 A: f9photos/iStockphoto; 28 B: Wolfgang Kaehler/age fotostock/Superstock, Inc.; 28 C: Reinhard Dirscherl/Getty Images; 28 D: Luis Castañeda/age fotostock; 28 E: Juan Carlos Vindas/Minden Pictures; 28 F: Brian Jannsen/age fotostock; 28 G: abalcazar/Getty Images; 28 H: RobertMayne/iStockphoto; 30 top left: marigold_88/iStockphoto; 30 top right: Hermsdorf/iStockphoto; 30 bottom: Ron Levine/Getty Images.

Maps by Jim McMahon.

Table of Contents

USA

Mexico

Where in the World Is Mexico?

Hola (OH-lah) from Mexico! That's how we say "hello" in Spanish. That's the language we speak in Mexico. We're Rosa and Pedro, your tour guides. We're twins. We have a lot of fascinating places and things to show you around our beautiful country. *¡Vámonos* (VAH-moh-nohs)! Let's go!

Fast Facts:

- **Mexico is located in North America. It is made up of 31 states and a federal district.**

- The Pacific Ocean lies on the west, and the Gulf of Mexico and the Caribbean Sea are on the east.

- There are two big deserts in the north. They are the Sonoran Desert and the Chihuahuan Desert.

- **At the southeastern end is the Yucatán Peninsula, known for its rain forest and white sandy beaches.**

- Two mountain ranges run down the east and west sides. Between the mountains is the Mexican Plateau. It has a lot of fertile soil, and much of the population lives there.

UNITED STATES

Tijuana

SONORAN DESERT

Ciudad Juárez

Rio Grande

Chihuahua

BAJA CALIFORNIA

Gulf of California

CHIHUAHUAN DESERT

Monterrey

Gulf of Mexico

Cabo San Lucas

Cancún

YUCATÁN PENINSULA

MEXICO

Colima

Mexico City

BELIZE

Acapulco

GUATEMALA

EL SALVADOR

PACIFIC OCEAN

N W E S

5

In Mexico City, you'll see houses painted just about every color you can imagine!

A picture of Mary, the mother of Jesus, hangs on a wall.

Home Sweet Home

We are from Mexico City, the capital of our country. We live with our *mamá* (mother) and *papá* (father), as well as two other brothers and sisters and our grandparents. It's really noisy in our house! But it's common in Mexico to have big, extended families living together.

Like most Mexican homes, our house is painted in bright colors—yellow, orange, green, and turquoise. Our family name, Sánchez, is carved on the top of our front door. There's no confusion about where we live! Inside our house, you'll see tile floors. Our colorful walls are filled with religious pictures and mini statues. Most people in Mexico are Catholic, and religion is very important to our family.

Adobe houses are usually smaller than the ones people are used to in the United States.

inside an adobe home

an adobe home

Our *tía* (aunt) and *tío* (uncle) live in a small village. Some houses there are a lot like ours. Others are more like tía and tío's. Their home is made of adobe bricks made from clay and straw with a straw roof. It is simple but comfortable, and it is always filled with the familiar smell of tía's cooking. Their home has one main room. It is used for cooking during the day and sleeping at night. Their whole family sleeps on straw mats. But we like to sleep on the hammocks that our uncle hooks to the wall when we visit.

Let's Eat!

You'll have many yummy food choices when visiting Mexico. There are some foods you might have heard of or eat at your house. To start our day, we have breakfast. A common breakfast meal consists of fried eggs, beans, and sauce on a *tortilla* (tor-TEE-yuh). A tortilla is a round, flat piece of bread made from ground corn or wheat flour. We call it the "bread of Mexico." Breakfast is very important, but lunch is our main meal. It's so big that we usually don't eat much for dinner.

So, what do we usually eat for our big lunch? *Quesadillas* (kay-sah-DEE-yahs) and *enchiladas* (en-chi-LAH-dahs) are popular favorites. A quesadilla is like a sandwich. For one kind of tasty quesadilla, we put cheese, beans, and chicken on top of a tortilla. Another tortilla is put on top to form the sandwich. Then the whole thing is cooked and eaten. Enchiladas are stuffed tortillas baked in sauce. Mamá makes those for us every weekend.

Tortillas

Quesadillas

Enchiladas

Tamales

Tamales (tah-MAH-lehs) and *tacos* are also popular. A tamale is a mixture of meat and corn dough wrapped in corn husks. Sometimes it is spicy. Other times, it is sweet and made with pineapples. That's our favorite kind. Tacos are crisp, fried tortillas that are stuffed with beans or meat and topped with lettuce, cheese, and chilies. Yum!

Mole

Flan

Some Mexican foods you might not know but will definitely want to try are *mole* (MOH-lay) and *flan* (FLAHN). Mole is a dish of turkey or chicken with a sauce of bitter chocolate, nuts, and hot spices poured on top. It's a local specialty. For dessert, we love our flan. It's a custard with a soft caramel topping. Each bite melts in your mouth!

9

Off to School

In our *escuela*, or school, all the students wear uniforms. We spend six years in elementary school, three in middle school (secondary), and three in high school (upper secondary). That's the same as most places in the United States. However, we don't get grades like A, B, or F. Instead, we get number grades—from 1 to 10. If we work hard, we get lots of 10s. Mamá and Papá prefer that!

In school, we learn to read and write in Spanish. That is our main language in Mexico. However, there are over 60 **indigenous** languages in our country, such as Nahuatl, Yucatec Maya, Zapotec, and Mixtec. These have been spoken in our country for hundreds, sometimes thousands, of years.

It's important to know how to count to 10 when you visit Mexico. Practice before you visit and you'll be an expert!

1	**uno** (*OO-noh*)
2	**dos** (*DOHZ*)
3	**tres** (*TRAYS*)
4	**cuatro** (*KWAH-troh*)
5	**cinco** (*SEEN-koh*)
6	**seis** (*SAYS*)
7	**siete** (*see-AY-tay*)
8	**ocho** (*Oh-choh*)
9	**nueve** (*noo-WAY-vay*)
10	**diez** (*dee-AYS*)

Spanish Accent Marks

In Spanish, we sometimes use accent marks above our vowels: *a, e, i, o, u*. For words ending in a vowel, *n*, or *s*, the second-to-last syllable is stressed (e.g., **to**do, **jo**ven, **lu**nes).

For words ending in all other consonants, we stress the last syllable (e.g., ani**mal**, ciu**dad**).

When one of these two rules is broken, we have to use an accent mark to help the reader know how to pronounce the word. An accent mark shows which part of the word should be stressed when saying it. Here are some examples: *in**glés**, **rá**pido*

We also use accent marks to distinguish words that sound the same, but have different meanings. Some examples are:

si (if) – *sí* (yes)

más (more) – *mas* (but)

The Legend of Maize

In school we learn a lot of <u>traditional</u> stories, such as legends and folktales. "The Legend of Maize" is one of our favorites. It tells the beginnings of our people's most important crop. Today, maize (corn) is found in most Mexican meals in one form or another—tortillas, stews, tamales, and more.

In ancient times the Aztec, a group of people who lived in Mexico from the 1300s to the 1500s, had a simple diet. They ate only the animals they could catch and the root vegetables they could dig out of the ground. But they wanted more. They wanted a great food they had heard about, but never found—maize. This great food was hidden behind the towering mountains that surrounded their city. It was out of reach. Only the gods would be able to get it for them.

Many gods tried. They used their powerful strength to move the mountains and create a pathway for the Aztecs. But each god failed. So the desperate Aztecs called out to the god Quetzalcoatl—the feathered serpent god who was part bird

A stone carving of Quetzalcoatl at an ancient pyramid in Mexico City

and part snake. Quetzalcoatl listened to the cries of the Aztec people. He heard the tales of other gods failing. Finally, he agreed to get the maize for them. But he made one promise. "I will get the maize not by force, but by using my wits. My brain is more powerful than any arms."

How would he do it? wondered the Aztec people. Quetzalcoatl had a plan! He changed into a tiny black ant. Only an ant would be able to sneak across the mountains and take the maize without being noticed. He knew the journey would be long and difficult. Each day Quetzalcoatl faced a new challenge. He was more tired than he had ever been. The trip was more dangerous than he had ever thought it would be. But day after day he overcame each challenge. Finally, Quetzalcoatl arrived behind the massive mountains. There he found the golden maize. But how could a tiny ant carry a giant stalk of maize across a mountain? Again Quetzalcoatl used his wits. He placed a small grain of maize in his mouth and headed back to the Aztec city.

Tiny step after tiny step, over the mountains he once more went. When he arrived at the Aztec city, the people flooded the streets in celebration. "Quetzalcoatl is our hero!" they shouted. Quickly the people planted the grain of maize. It grew and soon more grains were available. Over time fields of maize surrounded the city. The maize made the Aztecs a wealthy and powerful people. And they never forgot the little ant that used his giant wits to help them.

National Palace main square

Part of a mural by Diego Rivera

Torre Mayor

Touring Mexico

Mexico City: Capital City

Welcome to Mexico City, where we live. It's the capital of Mexico and our largest city. Almost 9 million people live here, with more than 20 million in the area surrounding it.

When you come here, you'll want to go first to the National Palace in the main square of Mexico City. Enslaved native people working for Spanish soldiers built this building in the 1500s. It's located where the palace of Montezuma, the last Aztec ruler, stood. The Aztecs were one of the main groups of people living in Mexico when the Spanish arrived. The builders even used some of the material from Montezuma's old palace to make the new one. Walk along the palace walls and enjoy the **murals** that tell the history of our country. They were painted by one of our greatest artists, Diego Rivera.

Not far from there, snap a photo of the Torre Mayor, one of the tallest buildings in Mexico. Take the elevator to the 52nd-floor observation deck (it only takes 36 seconds). From there, you can see for miles and miles.

This food stand in the Mercado Merced sells sweets!

Floating gardens

Ancient Aztec site

When you're done marveling at the view, grab your money and go to the Mercado Merced. At this big and busy market, you can buy fruits, vegetables, toys, household items, and more. If you're feeling adventurous, try some cactus, fried pig skins, or super-hot chili peppers.

After shopping, get ready for a ride on the canals in Xochimilco (zoh-chee-MEEL-koh). The Aztecs built the canals long ago. Hop on one of the colorful boats and you'll be amazed at the ancient floating gardens there. The Aztecs anchored rafts in the canals, piled them high with mud and grass, and then planted crops and flowers.

As you'll see, what's remarkable about our city is that modern buildings stand next to historic sites like these. In fact, ancient structures have been excavated right in the middle of Mexico City. You can also take a short car ride outside the city, where you'll find Aztec pyramids.

Chichén Itzá

Chichén Itzá

In addition to the Aztecs, another indigenous group called the Maya lived in Mexico. They also built a lot of great structures. Chichén Itzá is a famous Maya **temple** complex. Its biggest pyramid has 365 steps, one for each day of the year. You sure will be tired if you climb all those stairs! Chichén Itzá is located on the Yucatán **Peninsula**, which is home to many Maya people today. In fact, the Maya are our largest indigenous population. They have lived there for thousands of years.

Chichén Itzá was selected as one of the New Seven Wonders of the World. It has a huge ball court—545 feet (166 meters) long and 225 feet (69 m) wide—that would have been fun to play on. If someone whispers at one end, you can hear what the person says at the other end. Try it! Also, if you make a sound in the middle of the court, it makes nine echoes, echoes, echoes . . .

Mariachi band

Whale in Baja California

Cancún beach

Acapulco cliff diver

Other Must-See Places

There are lots of other places to visit in Mexico. Oaxaca (wah-HAH-kah) is home to colorful festivals and folk art. Another fun city is Guadalajara (gwah-dah-lah-HAH-rah), which holds a yearly festival for *mariachi* (mah-ree-AH-chee) music. The musicians play guitars, violins, and trumpets. You'll often see them strolling the streets wearing large-brimmed hats and colorful outfits. This city is a popular stop for **tourists**.

If swimming is more your thing, head to Acapulco and Cancún. These two cities have some of the world's best beaches. You'll also want to see the famous Acapulco cliff divers. Each day, they perform for tourists by jumping from cliffs into the sea below. But don't try it yourself! These divers are professionals. Another city for water lovers is La Paz. It is located on the Baja California Peninsula. We love hopping on a boat and going whale watching there.

Our Fascinating History

Our country has a long and interesting history. Many peoples have lived here. Beginning in about 1500 BCE, the Olmec people built huge stone heads. Some are as tall as 11 feet (3.3 m) and weigh 36,000 pounds (16,329 kilograms)! Starting in about 600 BCE, the Maya built pyramids and temples. They were also advanced in mathematics and astronomy. Between 1325 and 1519 CE, the Aztecs **conquered**

Aztec leader Montezuma meeting with Cortés

Timeline: Mexico's History

Maya statue

Aztecs

1500 BCE-400 CE

Olmec Empire
Crops such as corn and beans are first grown by the "mother culture."

1000-1500

Maya Empire
Great buildings, including pyramids, are built. Advances are made in science and math.

1325-1519

Aztec Empire
The Aztecs take over much of Mexico and create huge cities.

1519

Spanish Colonization
Spanish explorer Hernán Cortés arrives in Mexico. He conquers the land by 1521 as a Spanish colony called New Spain.

many groups in what is now Central Mexico. Their capital was Tenochtitlán (tehn-ahk-tiht-LAHN). Mexico City was built on this ancient city.

The native peoples' rule came to an end in 1521, when Spanish explorer Hernán Cortés conquered the lands for Spain. Three hundred years later, the Mexican people won freedom from Spain and founded the country of Mexico.

Mexican and U.S. forces battle

Mexico's flag

1810–1821
Fight for Independence
The Mexican War of Independence begins. Mexico becomes independent from Spain.

mid-1800s
Mexican-American War
Texas is claimed by the United States in 1845. The war ends in 1848.

1910–1917
Mexican Revolution
Mexico's longtime dictator, Porfirio Díaz, is overthrown after an armed uprising by the country's people.

Today
Modern Era
Mexico continues to be a powerful country, and it has strong ties to the United States.

It Came from Mexico

Thanks to Mexico, the world was introduced to everyone's favorite sweet treat—chocolate! It was first made in Mexico about 4,000 years ago. How? People ground cacao beans and added them to a mix of vanilla, honey, chili peppers, and water. It looked and tasted a bit like hot chocolate, but this special drink was reserved for rulers, wealthy nobles, and warriors. Sorry, none for us.

Chili peppers

Cacao beans and chocolate

Maize

Other foods we gave the world include squash, sweet potatoes, avocados, peppers, several kinds of beans, vanilla, chilies, tomatoes, and maize (corn).

You might have played a fun birthday game that was created in Mexico: the *piñata* (pin-YAH-tah)! Grab a stick and whack it until the stuffing falls out. This colorful container is usually filled with candy and small toys. It can be modeled to look like an animal, star, flower, or many other fun shapes. At our last party, we had a piñata shaped like a donkey. Hee-haw!

The Piñata-Breaking Song

We like to sing this song when playing with a piñata.

Dale, dale, dale	Hit it, hit it, hit it
No pierdas el tino	Don't lose your good aim
Porque si lo pierdes	Because if you lose it
Pierdes el camino	You'll lose the way

skull candy

Celebrate!

Everyone loves a holiday, and we have some fun ones in Mexico. Our favorite is the Day of the Dead, also called All Souls' Day. We celebrate it the first two days of November. It is to honor our **ancestors** who have died, but this is *not* a sad day. We have big parties and parades, paint our faces like skulls, and dress up in colorful outfits. We also get to eat skull-shaped candy—spooky and delicious!

Day of the Dead makeup

May 5

Cinco de Mayo
This holiday marks the day in 1862 that Mexicans bravely fought off French soldiers in the city of Puebla. This special day, celebrated on the fifth day of the fifth month, is also celebrated in the United States.

December 12

Our Lady of Guadalupe Day
This is the most religious holiday in Mexico, which we celebrate on December 12. It honors Our Lady of Guadalupe, the nation's patron saint.

September 16

Independence Day
We celebrate our freedom from Spain in 1810 on September 16 with big parades and fireworks.

Time to Play

Luchadores action figure

When it's time to play, we have lots of fun choices in Mexico. Little kids like to play with dolls. Some kids in our class like to play with action figures, especially those modeled after famous *luchadores* (loo-cha-DOR-ehs), or masked wrestlers. Los Vipers and El Matador are some of the most famous luchadores.

We also have some fun traditional games, such as Blind Hen. One player is blindfolded. The other players move around. The blindfolded player uses the other players' voices to try to find them. If a player is caught, that player is blindfolded and the game continues. Instead of saying things such as "go left" or "over here," we like to say "cluck, cluck" like a hen to help the blindfolded player find us.

El balero (EL bah-LEH-roh) is also common. It is a simple toy with a ball attached by string to a cup. The player must swing the string and try to get the ball inside the cup. The fewer the tries, the better. Our record is two tries. See if you can beat that!

El balero

People of all ages play fútbol in Mexico!

Kites are also popular toys, but nothing in Mexico beats a soccer ball. This is the sport that rules: *fútbol*. If you are a good player, you can become a national hero. *Béisbol* (baseball) and baloncesto (basketball) are also popular sports.

Like Spain, we have **bullfighting** in Mexico. It's an important tradition for us. Watch the matador wave his red cape and dodge the bull's deadly horns. This is a sport of skill and bravery. Some people prefer to watch it on TV. Rodeos are also popular in Mexico. Actually, they started here! At these cowboy competitions, we see daring horse-riding stunts, amazing roping feats, dangerous bull riding, and those fearless rodeo clowns.

25

You Won't Believe This!

Mexican jumping beans are a popular souvenir for tourists. These beans are seeds that grow on a shrub native to the Mexican desert. A moth larva burrows inside the seed. When the larva feels warmth, such as when someone holds the seed, it moves.

Every winter, about 30 billion monarch butterflies **migrate** to the forests in the state of Michoacán (mee-choh-ah-KAHN). They travel to avoid the harsh cold weather farther north.

Turning 15 years old is a big deal in Mexico for many girls. It is sometimes marked with a birthday celebration called a *quinceañera* (keen-seh-ah-NYEH-rah). It often includes a huge party, an important visit to church wearing a special dress, lots of dancing, and tons of fun.

There are about 3,000 volcanoes in Mexcio.

Lake Chapala in western Mexico is the country's largest lake. It is about one-third the size of Rhode Island.

Thousands of years ago, people in Mexico invented a game called *ollama*. It was like a mix of soccer, basketball, tennis, and squash. Two teams of seven players moved a hard rubber ball with their elbows, hips, and knees. The goal—get the ball through a small stone hoop way up high.

Ollama was a ritual with special religious meaning. At the end of the game, either the losing team captain or his entire team was sacrificed to the gods.

Guessing Game!

Here are some other great sites around Mexico. Can you guess which is which?

These Maya structures are just steps from the beach.
F

1. Tulum
2. Copper Canyon
3. Popocatépetl volcano
4. City of Mérida
5. Yucatán underwater caves
6. Palacio de Bellas Artes (Palace of Fine Arts)
7. Iztaccihuatl volcano
8. The ancient city of Teotihuacán

Take a look at the spectacular view at this landmark—which is deeper and wider than the Grand Canyon in the United States—by hopping off the train and crossing the bridge.
B

This "white city" in the Yucatán is a reminder of Mexico's past.
G

The giant pyramids of this abandoned city are a must-see.
A

Explore the underwater caves of the Yucatán.
C

H

The Palace of Fine Ar[t]s in Mexico City house[s] works by some of the most famous Mexica[n] artists and sculptors

This extinct volcano is known as the Sleeping Woman.
D

Called Popo, this is the second-highest volcano in Mexico. It has erupted about 30 times, spewing gas, ash, smoke, and steam. But most eruptions have been small. Whew!
E

How to Prepare for Your Visit

By now, you should be ready to hop on a plane to Mexico. Here are some tips to prepare for your trip around our country.

1 Before you come to Mexico, exchange your money. Here we use *pesos* (PAY-sohs). You'll need it to buy fun souvenirs.

2 If you have a big family like ours, most hotels have large family rooms with several beds.

3 If there's an emergency, you can call 9-1-1, just like in the United States.

4 Check to see if you need any shots before coming here. It's best to be **immunized** for illnesses such as typhoid and hepatitis. Also, if you're traveling to a part of Mexico where getting malaria is possible, ask your doctor for some special medicine.

5 Some places in Mexico are hot, hot, hot. Don't forget to pack your sunscreen, sunglasses, and a big hat. Also, wear lots of lightweight clothes made of cotton or linen.

6 Buses are a fast and cheap way to travel around our country. Plus, you get to see a lot more of the cities, villages, and countryside. Hop on and grab your camera.

7 *¡Chicle, chicle, chicle!* You'll hear children shouting this at airports, street markets, and almost everywhere tourists visit. What are they saying? Gum, gum, gum! You might want to buy a handful and chew away.

8 It's best to not drink the local tap water. Buy bottled water, even for brushing your teeth. Remember, ice cubes are made of water!

The United States Compared to Mexico

Official Name	United States of America (USA)	Estados Unidos Mexicanos (United States of Mexico)
Official Language	No official language, though English is most commonly used	Spanish
Population	325 million	122 million
Common Words	yes, no, excuse me, please, thank you, How are you?	sí, no, perdón, por favor, gracias, ¿Cómo estás?
Flag		
Money	dollar	peso
Location	North America	North and Central America
Highest Point	Mount McKinley	the volcano Citlaltépetl (or Orizaba)
Lowest Point	Death Valley	Laguna Salada
National Anthem	"The Star-Spangled Banner"	"Himno Nacional de Mexico"

So now you know some important and fascinating things about our country, Mexico. We hope to see you someday visiting our ancient  cities, splashing in the warm waters along our sandy beaches, or munching on one of our favorite festival foods. Until then, adiós. Good-bye.

Glossary

ancestors
(AN-ses-turz)
members of a family who lived long ago

bullfighting
(BUL-fye-ting)
a sport where a trained expert called a matador dodges the attacks of a charging bull

conquered
(KAHNG-kurd)
defeated and took control of an enemy or a territory

immunized
(IM-yoo-nized)
protected from a disease

indigenous
(in-DIH-jeh-nuhs)
native to a certain place

migrate
(MYE-grate)
to move to another area or climate at a particular time of year

murals
(MYOOR-uhlz)
large paintings done on a wall

peninsula
(puh-NIN-suh-luh)
a piece of land surrounded by water on three sides

temple
(TEM-puhl)
a building used to practice one's religion

tourists
(TOOR-ists)
people who are traveling and visiting a place for fun

traditional
(truh-DISH-uhn-uhl)
related to the customs, ideas, and beliefs that are handed down from one generation to the next

Index

Facts for Now

Visit this Scholastic website for more information on Mexico and to download the Teaching Guide for this series:

www.factsfornow.scholastic.com   Enter the keyword **MEXICO**

About the Author

Wiley Blevins lives and works in New York City. His greatest love is traveling and he has been to Mexico many times. Visiting Mexico gives him a fun  opportunity to practice his Spanish and explore the Maya and Aztec ruins. Wiley has written numerous books for kids, including others in this series.